Dear Mom —

I foun[d] ... while I w[as] ... Possible this s[omething] ... bought one to pass on ... and Andrew. Then it [came] on me that it would be a wonderful treat to get your ... to do one.

Please fill it up and send it back to me when you finish. I'll type copies the info for Sandy and Anta. I love you.

Perri

The Priceless Book of Mother's Wisdom

A Mother's Journal of Timeless Advice

ISBN 1-887655-61-1

Concept and Text by Criswell Freeman

WALNUT GROVE PRESS
Nashville, TN
(615) 256-8584

Printed in the United States of America
Book Design by Criswell Freeman & Sue Gerdes
Cover Design by Mary Mazer
Edited by Angela Beasley
1 2 3 4 5 6 7 8 9 10 • 96 97 98 99 00 01

Special thanks to Paula Balthrup, Angela Beasley,
Dick and Mary Freeman, Margaret and Jack Queen.

This Book Records
The Wisdom Of

_____

A Message to Mothers

Dear Mom,

Would you like to pass along some sound advice to future generations? Here's your chance. On the following pages, record your favorite sayings, quotations, life-lessons and memories. As you do, you'll be preserving a body of wisdom the family will treasure now, and for years to come.

If the task of writing your thoughts seems challenging, don't worry. There's no hurry. Simply keep this book in a handy place. Then, when you hear yourself saying something profound, reach for a pencil and write it down.

This book is organized in chapters which are designed to prompt your creativity. Feel free to make additions and modifications as needed. After all, this is your book.

Be sure to keep this little volume in a safe place, because it's destined to become one of your family's most treasured possessions.

Mother's Dedication
This Book Is Dedicated to

_____

_____

_____

Mother's Favorite Sayings

On the following pages, jot down your favorite sayings, humorous stories, and quotations. These maxims may be yours or they may be the words of relatives, friends, or famous people.

Pay special attention to the sayings you heard as a child. Your children – and their children – will find them fascinating.

Mother's Favorite Sayings

Mother's Favorite Sayings

Mother's Favorite Sayings

Mother's Favorite Sayings

_____

_____

_____

_____

_____

_____

_____

_____

_____

_____

_____

_____

Mother's Favorite Sayings

_____

_____

_____

_____

_____

_____

_____

_____

_____

_____

_____

_____

_____

_____

_____

_____

Mother's Favorite Verses

Whether it's a poem, a song, a jingle, a hymn or a nursery rhyme, great truth often hides inside simple couplets. On the following pages, record some of *your* favorite verses.

Mother's Favorite Verses

Mother's Favorite Verses

Mother's Favorite Verses

Mother's Favorite Verses

Mother's Favorite Verses

Lessons I Learned
From My Family

Even the most insightful mom has much
to learn from her family. You learned lessons
as a child that have served you well in later
years. Take note of the those lessons and
share them on the following pages. Feel free
to include tales from childhood and beyond.
The family will be educated and entertained,
but not necessarily in that order.

Lessons From My Family

Lessons From My Family

Lessons From My Family

Lessons From My Family

_____

_____

_____

_____

_____

_____

_____

_____

_____

_____

_____

_____

_____

_____

_____

_____

_____

Lessons From My Family

Important People
In My Life and
What They Taught Me

All of us have been guided by special friends, teachers and mentors. Here is a chance to commit some of these lessons to paper.

Lessons From Important People

Lessons From Important People

Lessons From Important People

Lessons From Important People

Lessons From Important People

The Lessons I Learned
From The
Most Unexpected Sources

Life teaches us in surprising ways. Share the lessons you learned from the most unexpected sources. Maybe you'll save future generations some unpleasant surprises.

Lessons From Unexpected Sources

Lessons From Unexpected Sources

Lessons From Unexpected Sources

Mother's Advice

Reach back for your best motherly insights, and share them on the following topics.

Mother's Advice About ...
Honesty

Motherly Advice About ...
Courage

Mother's Advice About ...
Perseverance

Mother's Advice About ...
Courtesy

_____

_____

_____

_____

_____

_____

_____

_____

_____

_____

_____

_____

Mother's Advice About ...
Love

Mother's Advice About ...
Marriage

Mother's Advice About ...
Work

Mother's Advice About ...
Having Fun

Mother's Advice About ...
Faith

Mother's Advice About ...
Tough Times

Mother's Advice About ...
Priorities

Mother's Advice About ...
Money

Mother's Advice About ...
Hope

Mother's Advice About ...
Change

_____

_____

_____

_____

_____

_____

_____

_____

_____

_____

_____

_____

_____

_____

_____

Mother's Advice About ...
The Passage of Time

_____

_____

_____

_____

_____

_____

_____

_____

_____

_____

_____

_____

_____

_____

_____

_____

_____

_____

_____

Homemaking Hints

Although roles are rapidly changing, mothers have traditionally managed the home. Here is a chance to share some of your hard-earned wisdom on the topics that follow.

Mother's Hints on ...
Raising Children

Mother's Hints on ...
Nutrition and Cooking

Mother's Hints on ...
Housekeeping

Mother's Hints on ...
Making Ends Meet

Mother's Hints on ...
Hospitality

Mother's Hints on ...
Keeping Peace in the Family

Mother's Hints on ...
Making Time for Yourself

Mother's Favorite Memories

Here's an opportunity to record some of your favorite memories. After all, if you don't, who will?

Mother's Memories About ...
Grammar School

Mother's Memories About ...
Teenage Years

Mother's Memories About ...
Courtship

Mother's Memories About ...
Old Folks

Mother's Memories About ...
Childbirth

Mother's Memories About ...
Raising Children

Mother's Memories About ...
Vacations

Mother's Memories About ...
Holidays

Mother's Memories About ...
Best Friends

Mother's Memories About ...
Family

Mother's Favorite
Memories

Mother's Favorite
Memories

Mother's Favorite
Memories

_____

_____

_____

_____

_____

_____

_____

_____

_____

_____

_____

_____

_____

_____

_____

_____

Motherly "Firsts"

There's a first time for everything. Here's your chance to record some of those special moments.

First Thing You Remember

_____

_____

_____

_____

_____

_____

_____

First Home You Remember

_____

_____

_____

_____

_____

_____

_____

First Day at School

_____

_____

_____

_____

_____

_____

_____

First Date

_____

_____

_____

_____

_____

_____

_____

First Kiss

First Job

First Home of Your Own

_____

_____

_____

_____

_____

_____

_____

First Day as a Mother

_____

_____

_____

_____

_____

_____

_____

Other Important "Firsts"

Mother's Message
to the Family

Okay, Mom, here's your chance to send
a message to the family.

Mother's Message to the Family

Mother's Message to the Family

_____

_____

_____

_____

_____

_____

_____

_____

_____

_____

_____

_____

_____

_____

_____

Mother's Message to the Family

A Mother's Legacy:
How I Want
To Be Remembered

How I Want To Be Remembered

How I Want To Be Remembered

How I Want To Be Remembered

Facts About Mother:

Full Name: _____

Date of Birth: _____

Place of Birth: _____

Mother: _____

Father: _____

Siblings: _____

_____

_____

_____

Marriage: _____

_____

_____

Children: _____

_____

_____

_____

More Information About Mother and the Family

_____

_____

_____

_____

_____

_____

_____

_____

_____

_____

_____

_____

_____

_____

_____

More Information About Mother
and the Family

More Information About Mother and the Family

More Information About Mother
and the Family